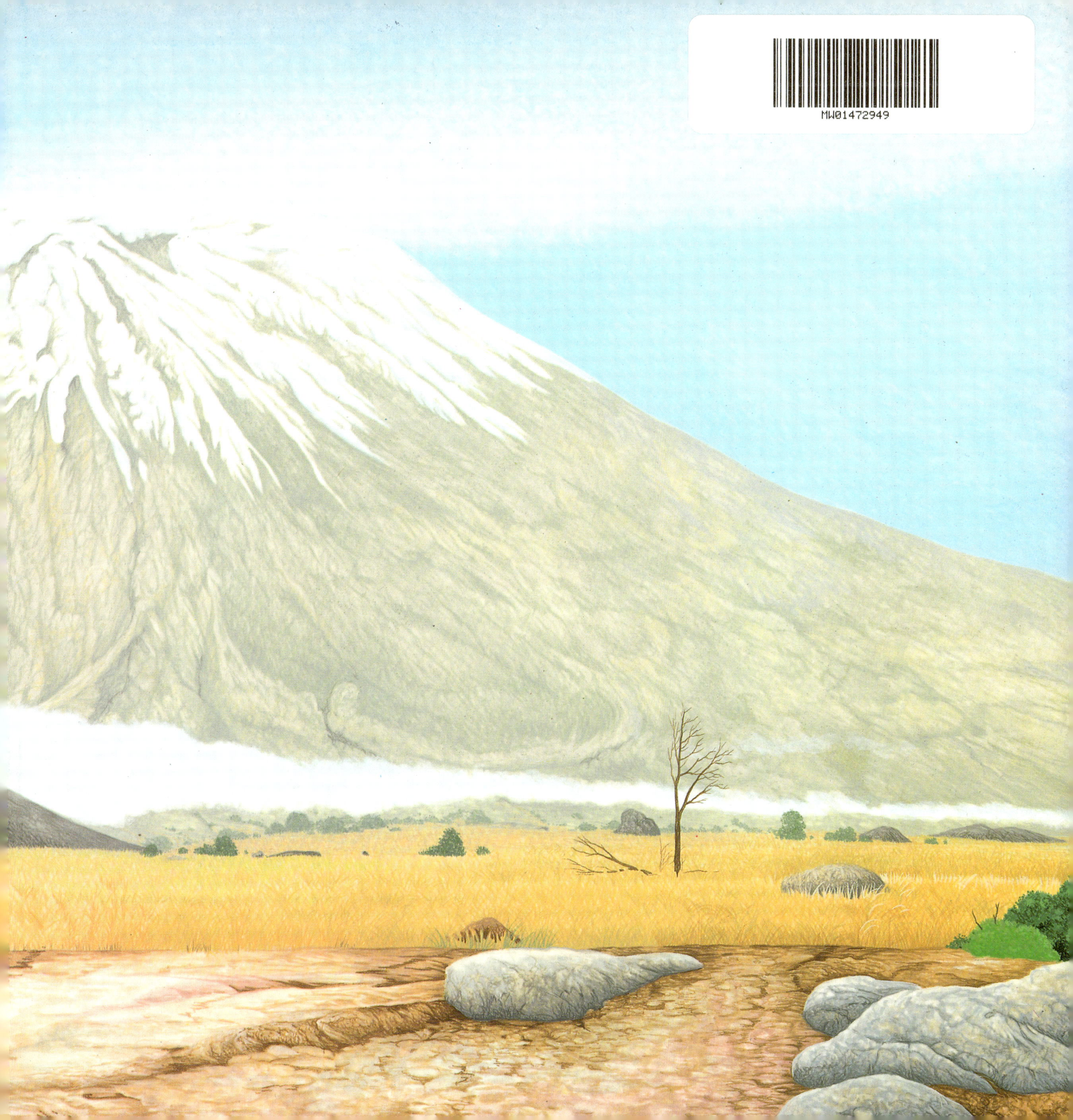

The Sierra Club, founded in 1892 by John Muir, has devoted itself to the study and protection of the earth's scenic and ecological resources — mountains, wetlands, woodlands, wild shores and rivers, deserts and plains. The publishing program of the Sierra Club offers books to the public as a nonprofit educational service in the hope that they may enlarge the public's understanding of the Club's basic concerns. The Sierra Club has some sixty chapters in the United States and in Canada. For information about how you may participate in its programs to preserve wilderness and the quality of life, please address inquiries to Sierra Club, 730 Polk Street, San Francisco, CA 94109.

Story and illustrations copyright © 1991 by Ilex Publishers Ltd.
Introduction copyright © 1991 by Sierra Club Books and Little, Brown and Company (Inc.)

All rights reserved. No part of this book may be reproduced in any form or by any electronic or mechanical means, including information storage and retrieval systems, without permission in writing from the publisher, except by a reviewer who may quote brief passages in a review.

First edition

Library of Congress Cataloging-in-Publication Data

Sackett, Elisabeth.
    Danger on the African grassland/Elisabeth Sackett: illustrations by Martin Camm. — 1st ed.
    p. cm.
    Summary: A young rhinoceros and his mother, who is shot by hunters on the African grasslands, flee for their lives, ultimately arriving at a reserve where they can sleep in peace and safety.
    ISBN 0-316-76596-1
    1. Rhinoceros — Juvenile fiction. [1. Rhinoceros — Fiction.]
I. Camm, Martin, ill. II. Title.
PZ10.3.S127Da1   1991
[E] — dc20   90-53701

Sierra Club Books/Little, Brown children's books are published by
Little, Brown and Company (Inc.) in association with Sierra Club Books.

10 9 8 7 6 5 4 3 2 1

Published simultaneously in Canada by
Little, Brown & Company (Canada) Limited

Printed in Spain

Danger on the African Grassland

by Elisabeth Sackett

Illustrations by Martin Camm

Introduction by Cynthia Overbeck Bix

Sierra Club Books | Little, Brown and Company
San Francisco | Boston · Toronto · London

Introduction

In southern Africa are lands called savannas, which are covered in tall grasses and dotted here and there with trees. During the rainy season, the grasses grow green, gold, and brown, and the water holes are full. When the dry season comes, water is scarce and the grasses are swept by fire.

Here lives an amazing variety of animals — lions, giraffes, zebras, and more. Of all the animals that live on the savannas, perhaps the strangest looking is the rhinoceros. This big, lumbering creature looks as if it were armor-plated. Its hide, or skin, is tough and thick, and on its head are two curved, pointed horns.

Lions and other hunting animals rarely bother the big, tough rhinoceros. Sadly, its greatest enemy is humankind. Over many years, people have hunted and killed so many rhinos that they are now in danger of disappearing forever. The rhino's horn and other body parts have long been used in Asia to make various medicines. And in some areas of the Middle East, the horns are prized as handles for ceremonial daggers.

Today the killing of rhinoceroses is outlawed in most places. In Africa, rhinos are protected in national parks and game reserves. But the prices people will pay for rhinoceros horns are so great that poachers ignore the law and kill rhinos anyway. Often the game wardens cannot stop them in time.

Conservationists are currently trying to persuade people not to use rhinoceros horns. At the same time, scientists are working to increase the rhino population by careful breeding in protected places. In some areas, progress is being made and herds are being restored. With the efforts of concerned people everywhere, perhaps one day the rhinoceros will be able to roam the grasslands in peace once again.

A fiery sun shone above the dusty African grassland. The thornbushes and flat-topped trees shimmered in the fierce heat. A lizard scuttled under a rock as he felt the ground shake beneath him. He waited there, watching cautiously as the pounding of feet grew louder.

A rhinoceros was moving heavily across the plain, stopping occasionally so that her small calf could catch up with her. Although he was trying very hard to keep trotting beside his mother, his legs were short, and he kept falling behind. By midday he was hot and thirsty, as well as very tired.

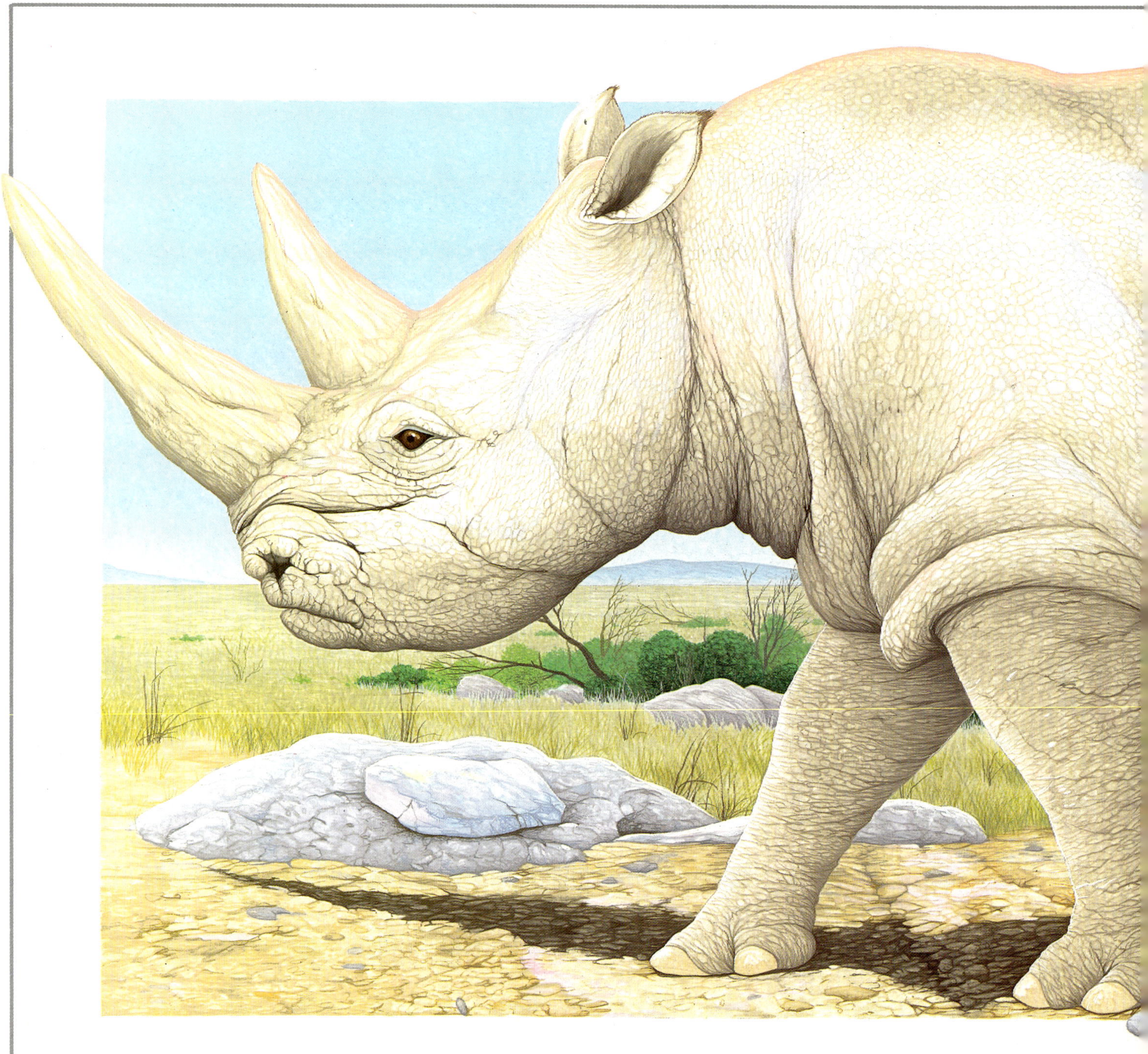

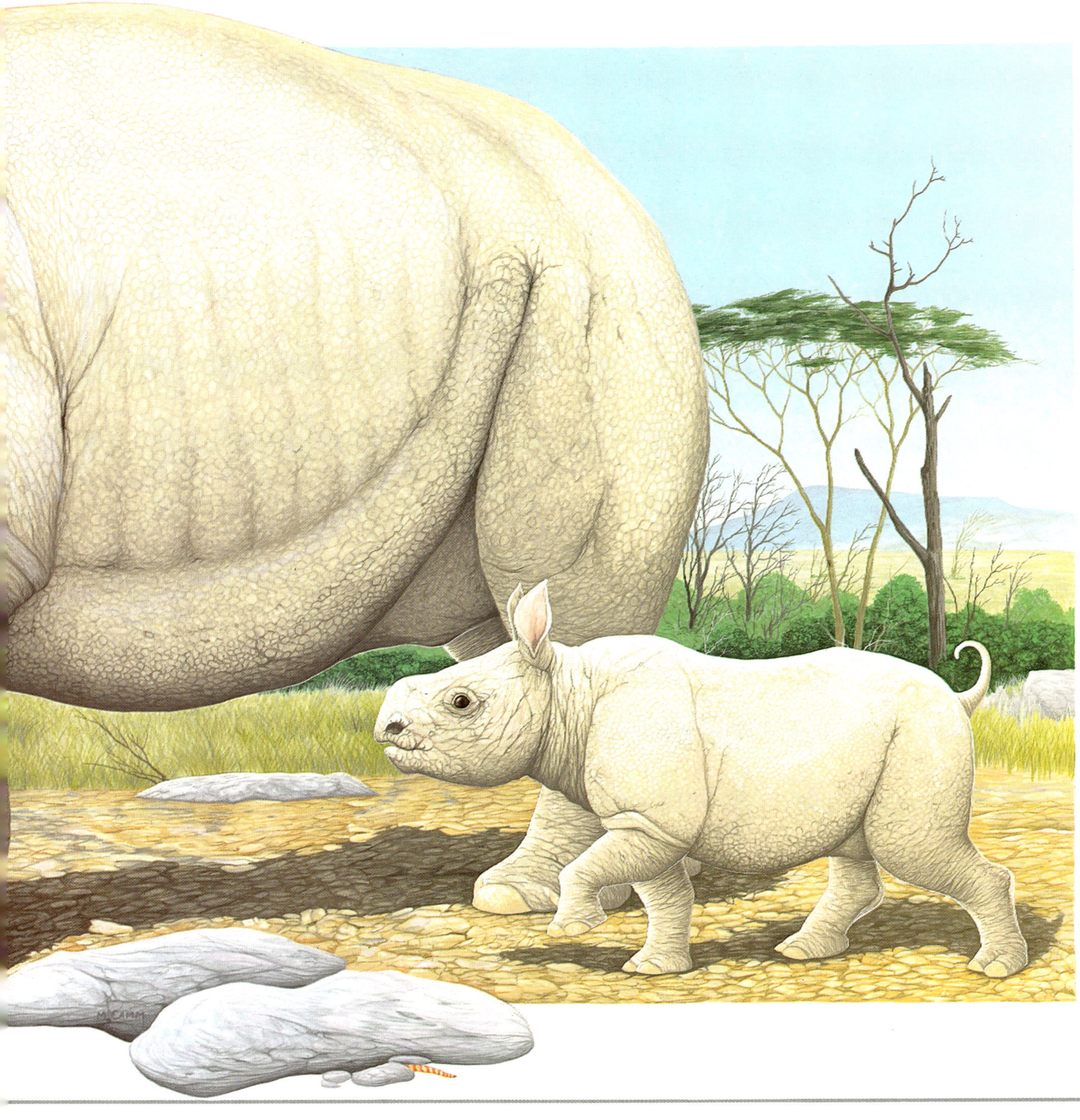

The mother rhinoceros stood still until her son came to her side. At dawn that day she had been feeding with him in the silence and freshness of the morning. Then, faintly through the still air, she had heard the sound of a jeep, the roar and rattle as it crossed the grassland. The mother rhinoceros had felt afraid. She knew who rode in the jeep: humans who came to the grassland to shoot rhinoceroses.

She had pushed hard at her calf, grunting her fear, and had started running over the plain to escape the humans and their guns. She now turned her head and nuzzled him. He had traveled such a long way that day and had tried so hard to keep close to her on his stubby legs.

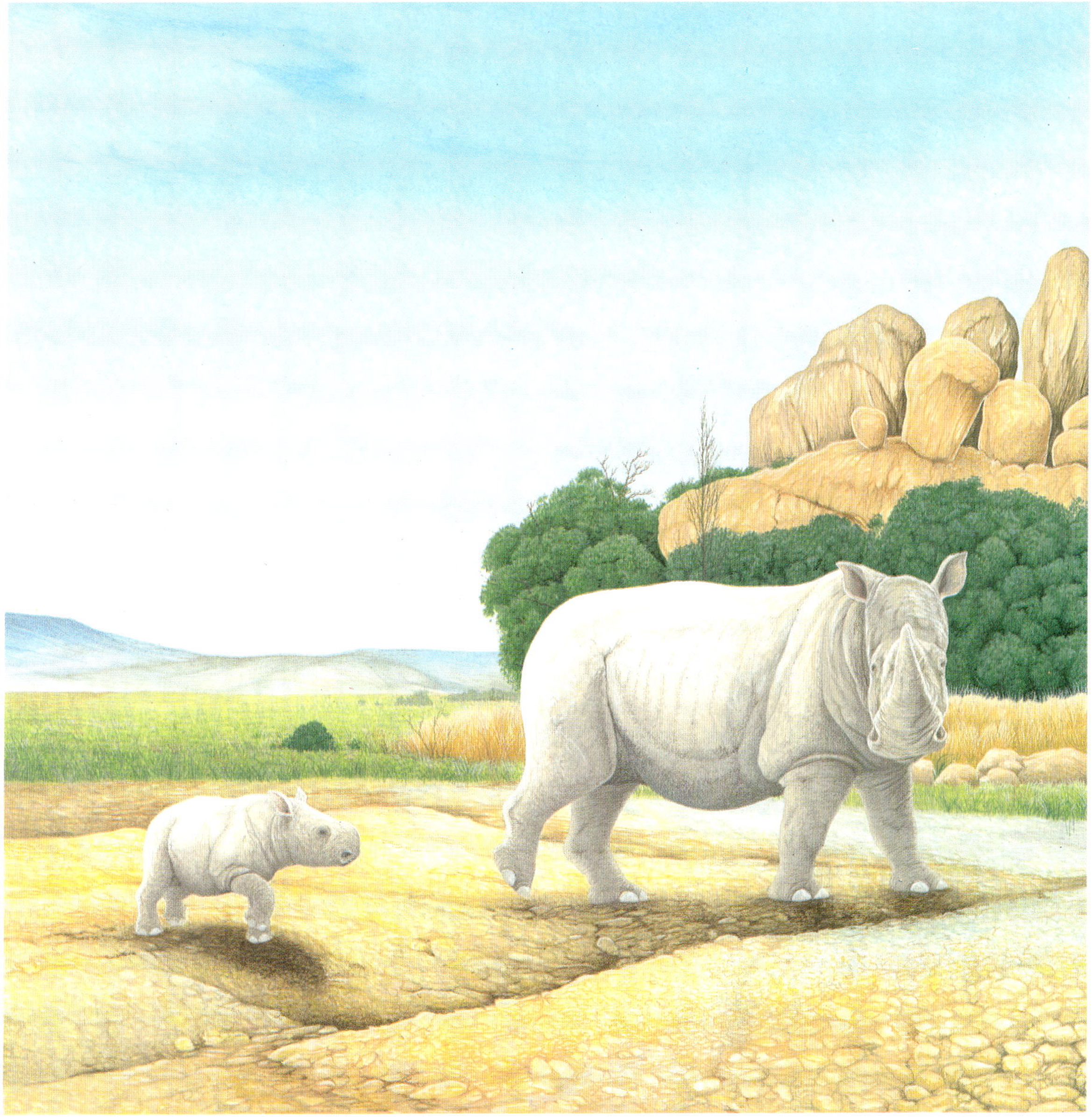

Pausing for a moment, the mother rhinoceros glanced uneasily around her. Had they come far enough?

The little calf peered around his mother's legs and saw the grassland stretching far into the distance. Giraffes, tall and graceful, were feeding on the topmost shoots of trees. Herds of zebra grazed on the coarse grass, their black-and-white-striped bodies shining in the sunlight. A family of warthogs searched beneath the dry earth for tender roots.

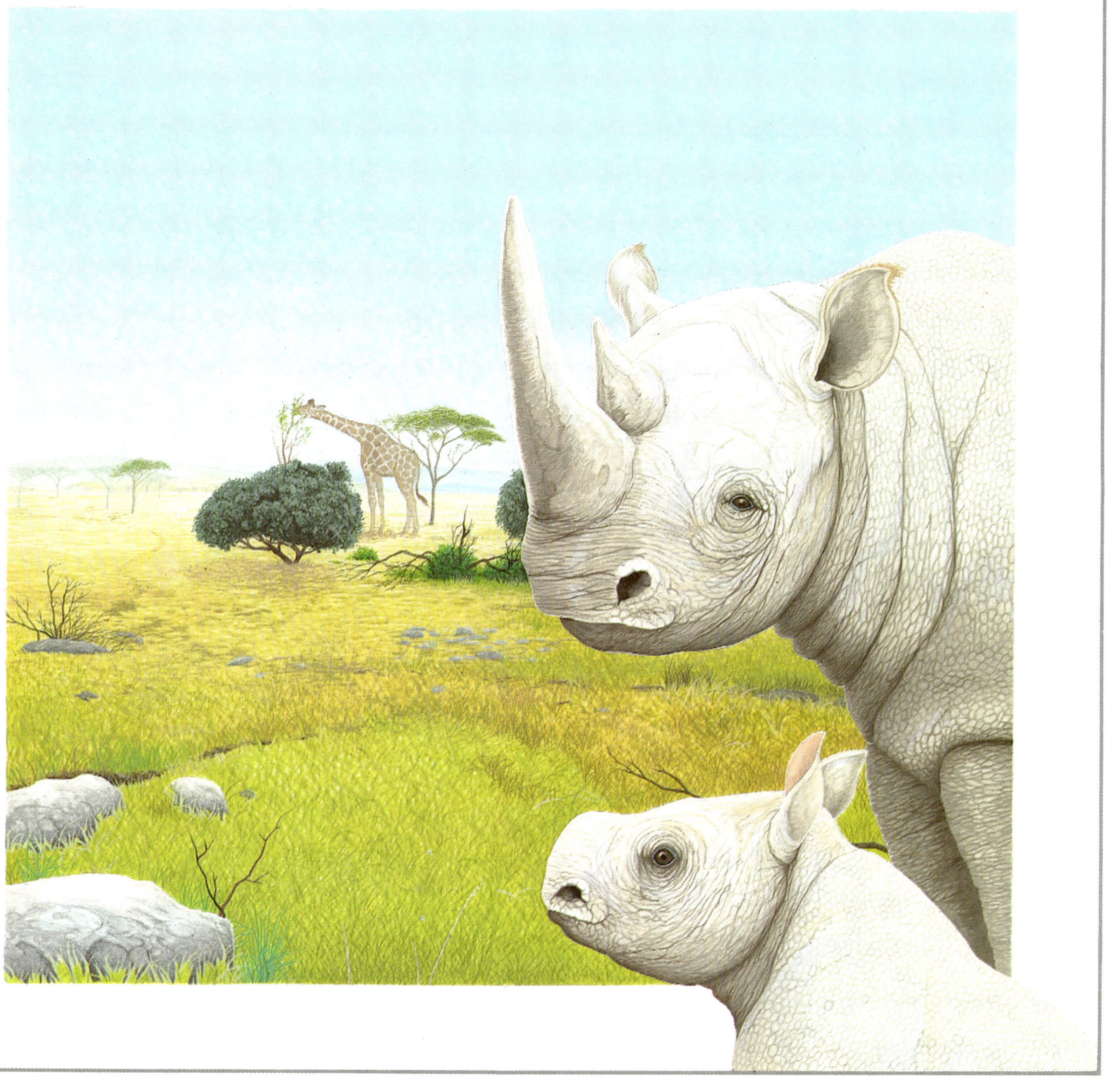

Suddenly the still, hot air was shattered by the sound of rifle shots resounding over the plain. Moments later, the grassland shook with the thunder of hooves. The animals that had just been feeding peacefully were now stampeding.

A shrill, screaming sound whizzed past the small rhinoceros — and his mother staggered forward, grunting with pain. Confused and afraid, the little calf stood very close to her as the other animals galloped around them.

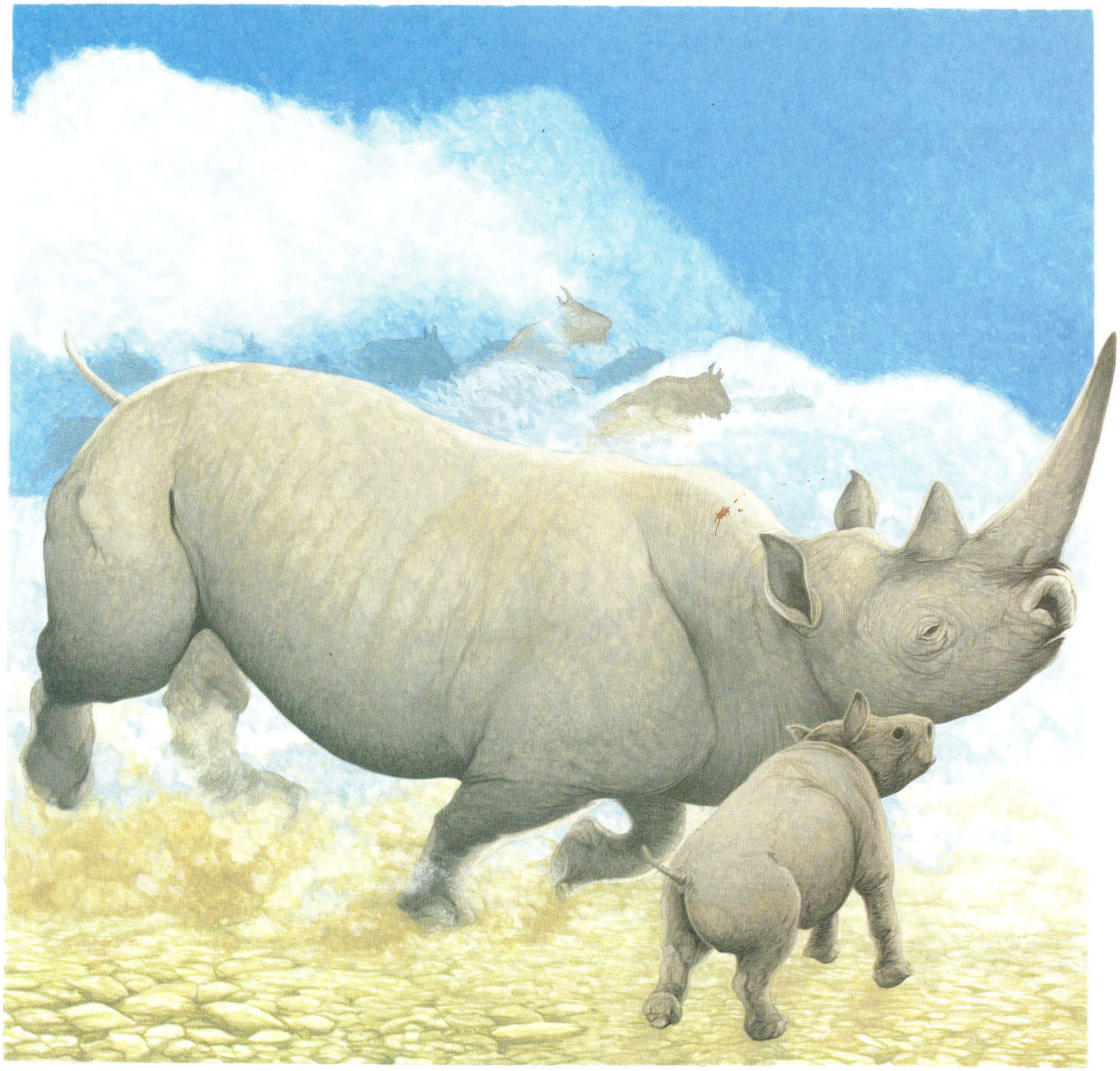

The mother rhinoceros hesitated, tossing her head. She was badly injured and needed to rest, but she knew there was only one chance for survival. Calling to her son, she started after the fleeing animals.

As the mother and calf ran, the clouds of dust kicked up by the running herds choked the young rhinoceros. He stumbled and fell to the ground but quickly scrambled back to his feet and hurried after his mother as fast as his small legs could manage.

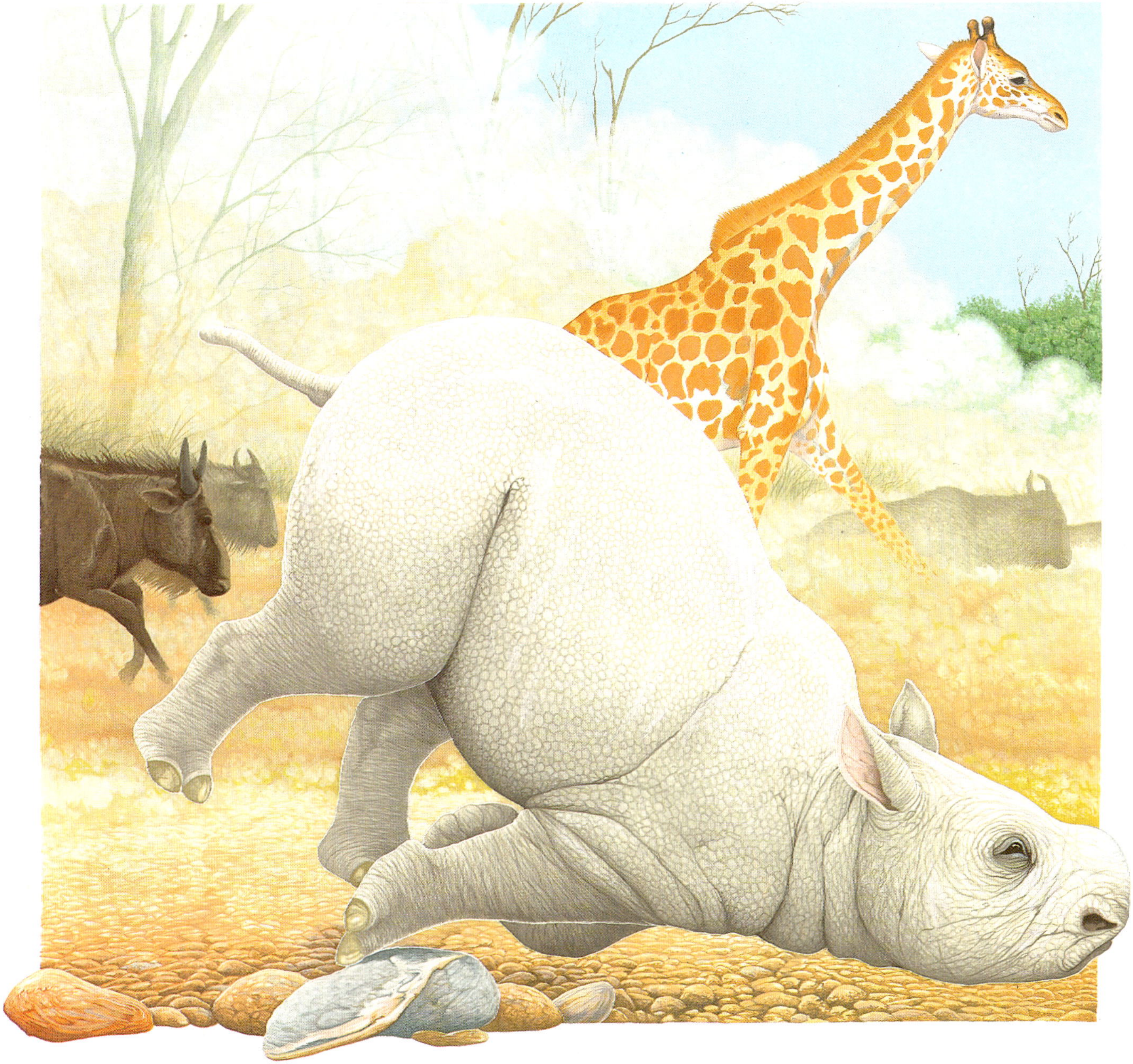

The animals continued their flight through the afternoon. The mother rhinoceros kept up with the others for many miles, but pain and loss of blood finally exhausted her, and she collapsed to the ground. Trembling with fear, the little calf nestled close to his mother, but she did not respond to his whimpers.

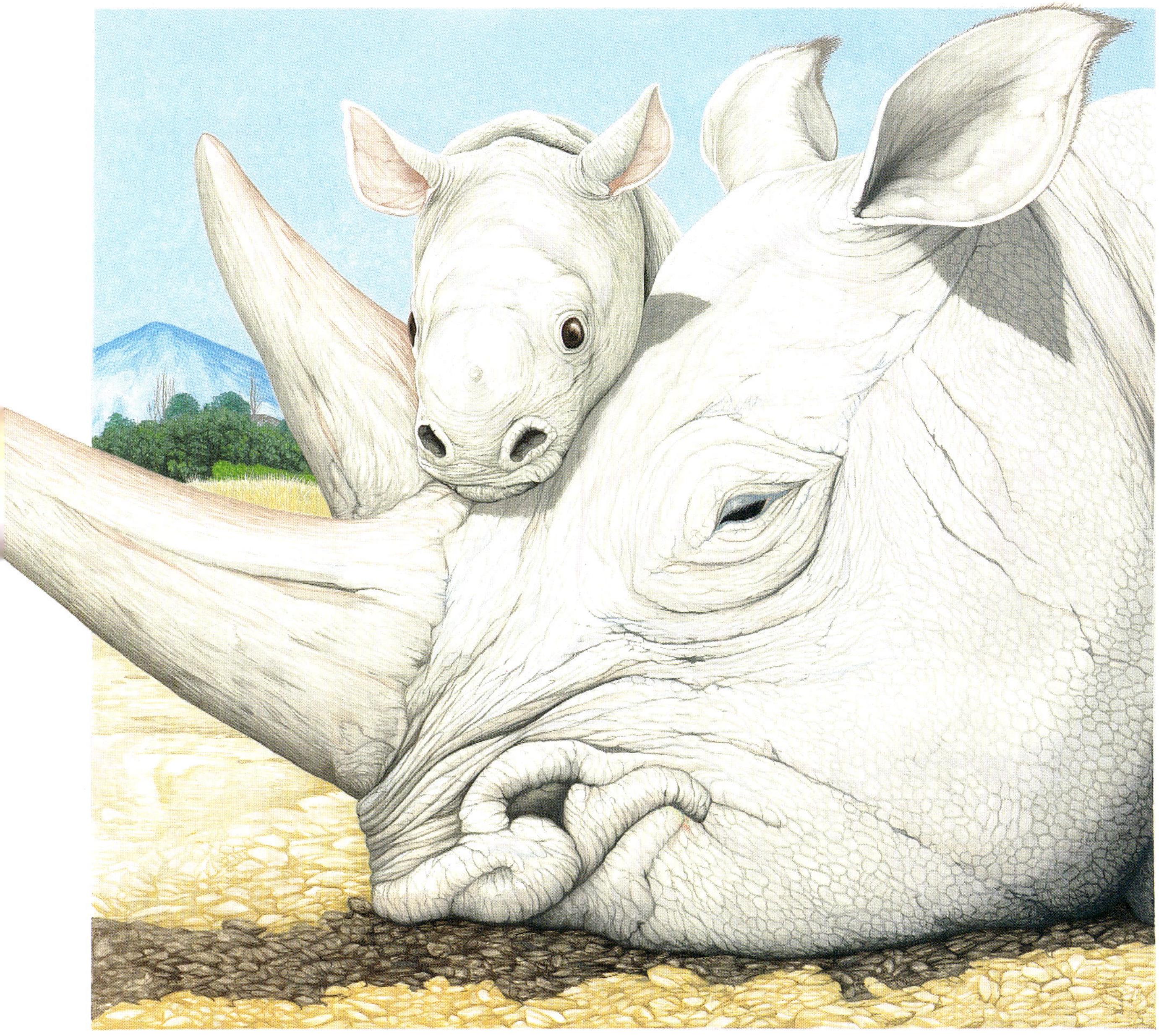

For several minutes she lay very still on the dry, dusty earth. Then, with tremendous effort, she got to her feet and started off again across the grassland. She walked so slowly now that the little calf had no trouble staying beside her. The other animals had moved far into the distance and were barely visible among clouds of dust.

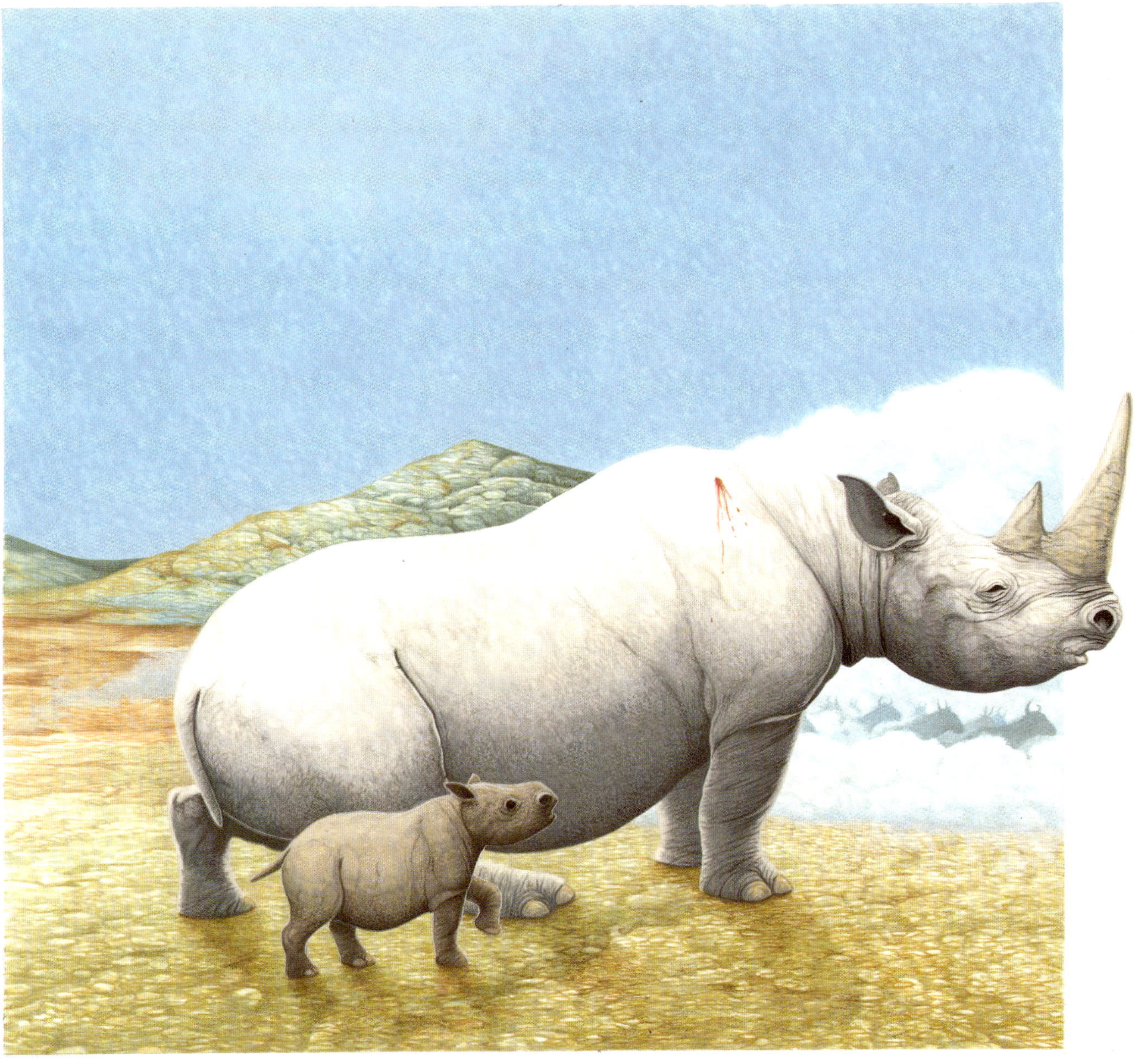

At last the mother rhinoceros and her son came to where the other animals were grazing or resting. The sun had become red-gold and was now sinking quickly in the west. As it hung for a moment on the horizon, the animals stood quite still. Tall giraffes, stocky zebras, graceful gazelles — all looked black against the glowing sky. Then they all drifted slowly forward, as if in search of something.

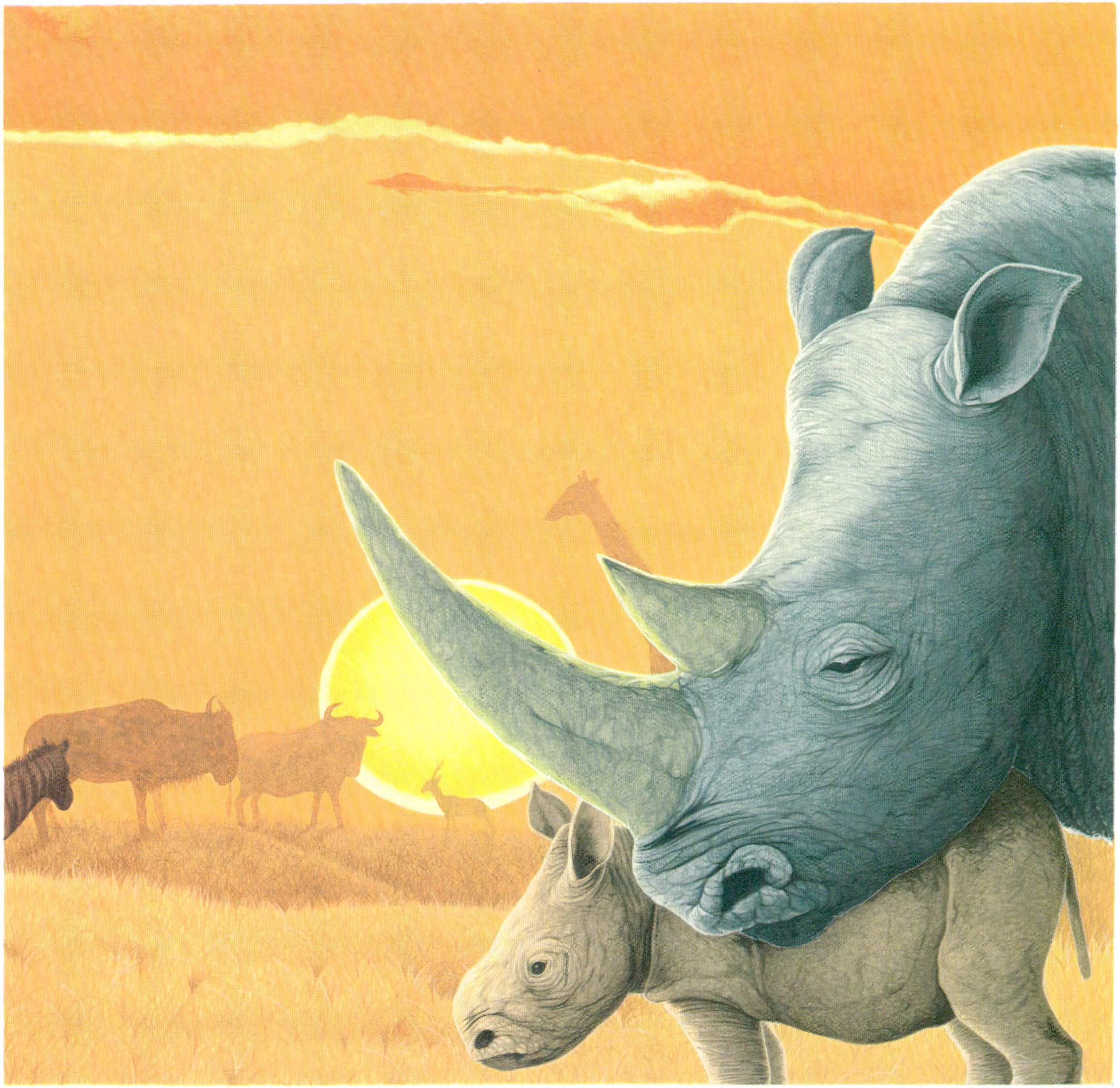

The mother rhinoceros lifted her head and sniffed the air. She could smell water! In the last glow of the setting sun, she moved toward the water hole, pushing her calf in front of her, and soon they both plunged in. As the little one splashed and drank in the shallow water, the mother rhinoceros rolled gently from side to side in the cool mud, smothering her painful wound.

At last the mother rhinoceros felt strong enough to eat. She stood up, shook the mud from her sides, and climbed out of the water hole in search of tender grass. The little rhinoceros followed his mother's example and trotted off close behind her.

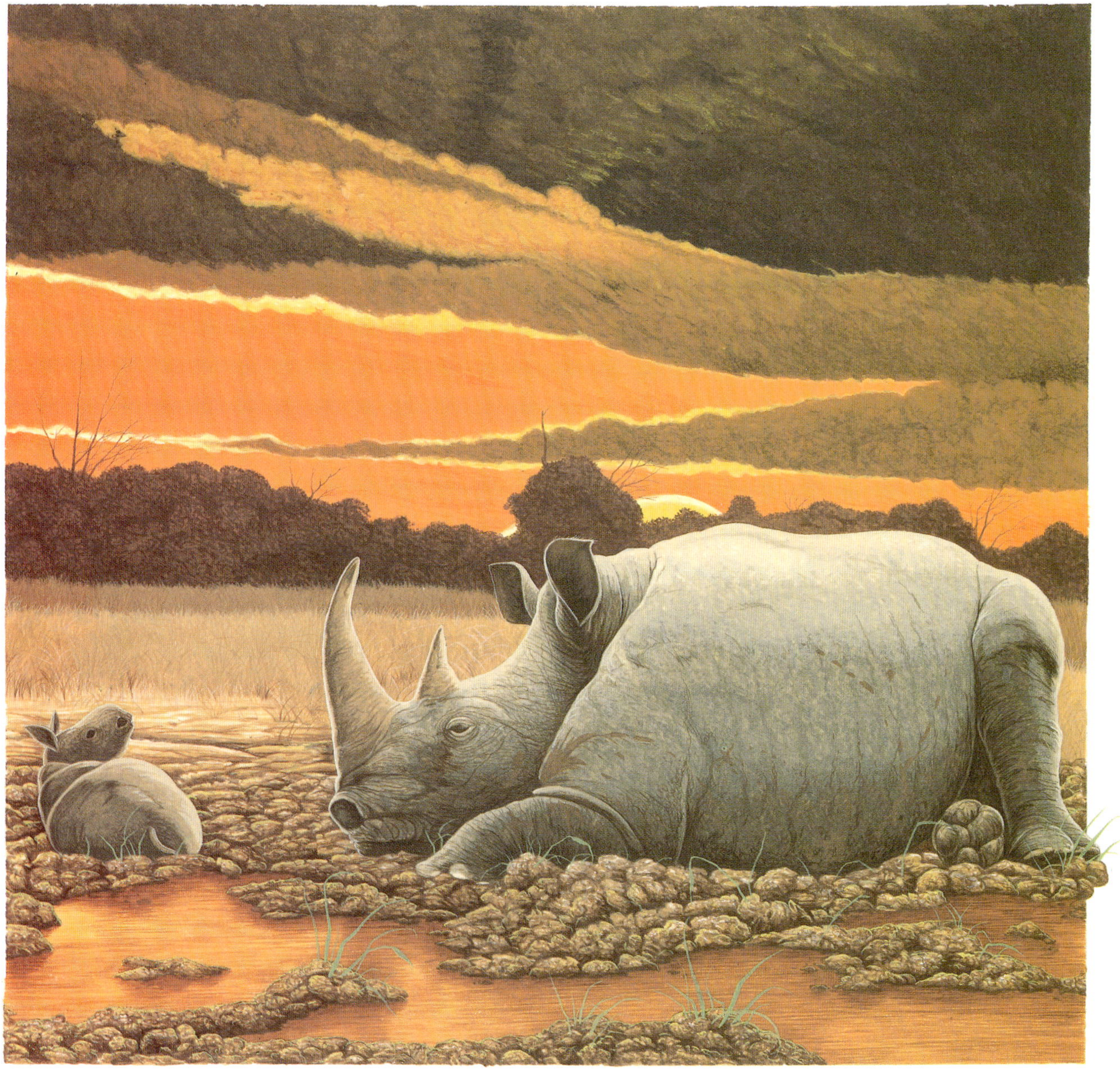

When they had eaten their fill, the mother rhinoceros lay down to sleep with the little calf tucked against her body. At last the small rhinoceros closed his round black eyes and fell asleep, too.

High above them, in the black velvet sky, a bright moon shed its silver light over the reserve, where all the animals could sleep in peace and safety.

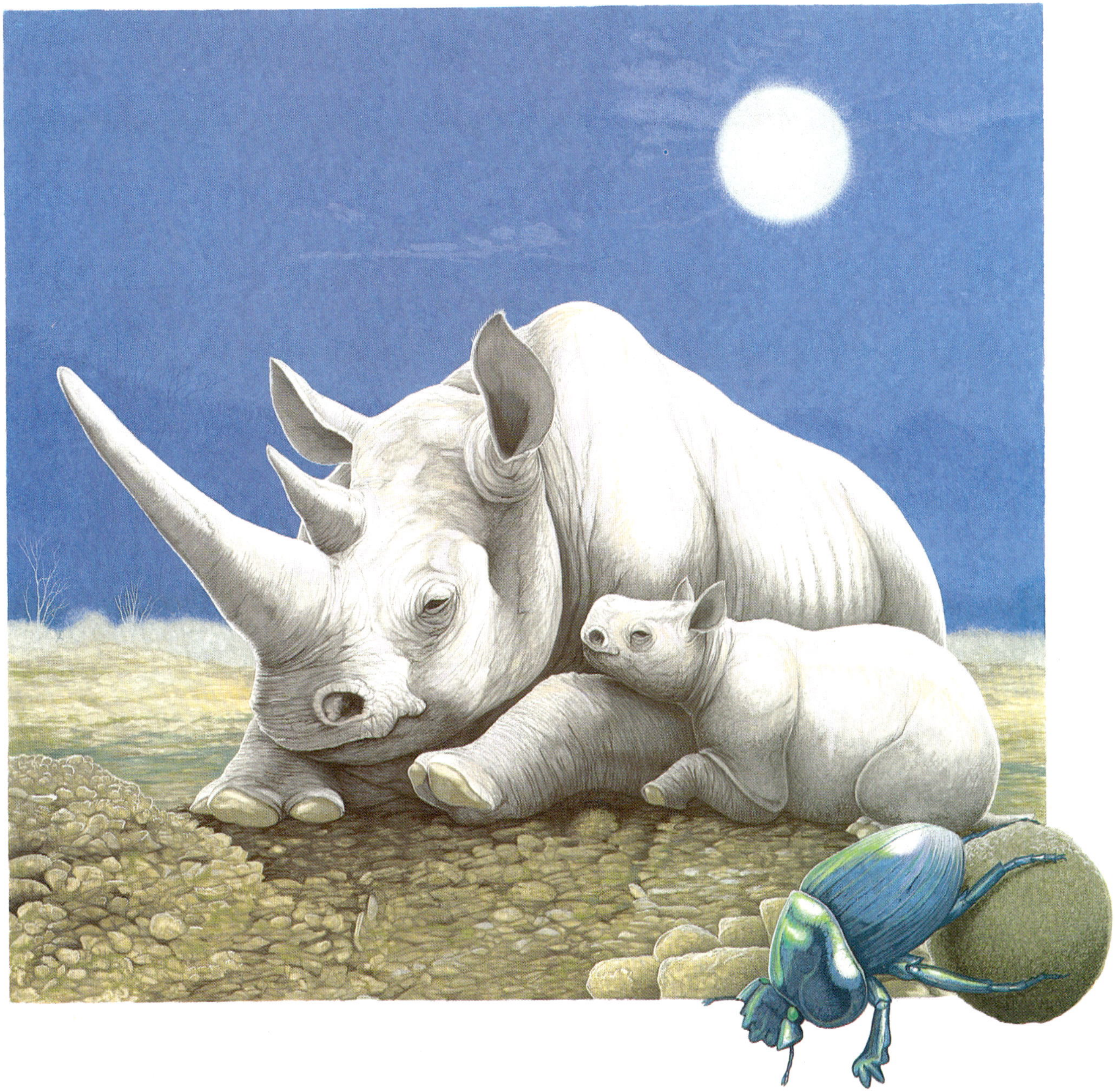

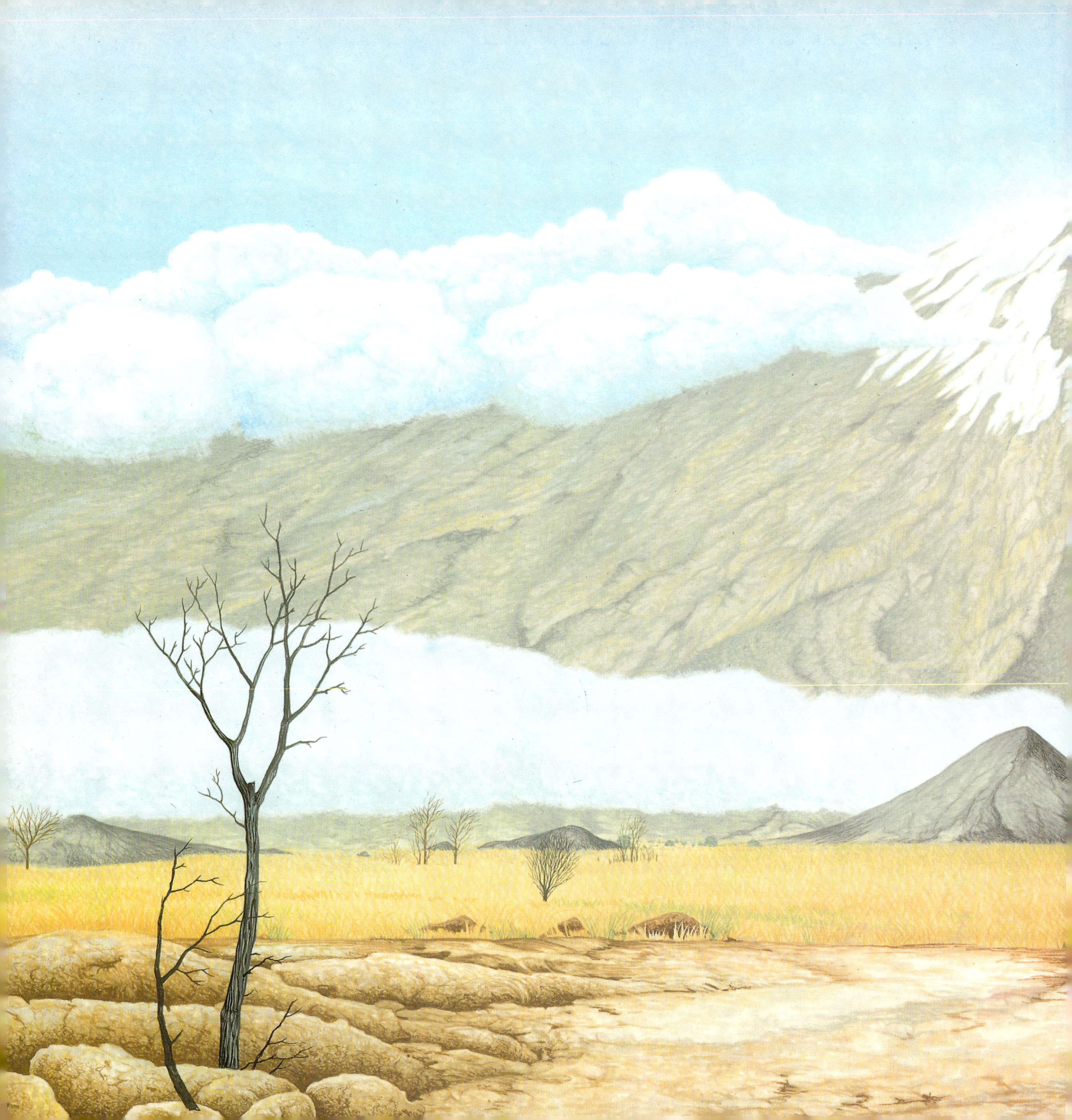